Printed in Great Britain
by Amazon

52306291R00068